ALL THE JOURNEYS
I NEVER TOOK

Rebecca Tantony

Burning Eye

BurningEyeBooks
Never Knowingly
Mainstream

Copyright © 2017 Rebecca Tantony

This edition published by Burning Eye Books 2017

www.burningeye.co.uk

@burningeyebooks

Burning Eye Books
15 West Hill, Portishead, BS20 6LG

ISBN 978 1 90913 698 4

Cover design & illustrations by Anna Higgie

ALL THE JOURNEYS
I NEVER TOOK

CONTENTS

Then

Here

Now

Lost

Far

Near

Found

THEN

When did I start running back on myself? Retracing and recalling the homes of my youth. Five different houses, all filled with escape.

CIRCLES

In the discos of our childhoods
we danced in the end
of each school year,
the music a flood of futures.

While above, the cycle
of the sun and earth in orbit
would foxtrot around
one another, always moving in the echo

of what had been before.
Below, Ace of Base poured
through the speakers,
and I, too, would trace rotations

with my waist,
a map drawn by hip bone,
that spoke of destinations
in the light-years to come.

We were all outlining futures
with the circle of our bodies.
Journeys we were yet
to move towards.

GROWING

When I was a child my mother made my clothes.
Her already crumpled hands passed thread
through needles. She said, 'We can't afford to
buy much, but we can make ourselves
out of nothing.'

Aged twelve I wear a polka-dot dress
and matching headband, while the other
dance-class girls are stuffed into tight Lycra,
belly tops that show off protruding rib bones.
I stand back

of the class, embarrassed that I can't move
as gracefully as those front-row girls.
All puppy-fat folded into that dress,
I squeak across the lino floor. When finished,
whilst waiting for

our parents to collect us, we huddle,
a cigarette smoked and passed
leaves a memory on my clothes long after
I have undressed. My mother bundles me
into the back

of her broken car and I press my face against
the window, stare at those disappearing girls.
Their lipsticked mouths like a trail behind our
leaving, their self-assurance somewhere too distant for
me to grasp.

NOVA

---

*'You can search throughout the entire universe looking for
someone who is more deserving of your love and affection
than you are and that person is not to be found anywhere.'*
Siddhārtha Gautama

I just can't stop growing past the memory
of trying to French-kiss my own hand.
Those lip-marks smacked. How can you remove
yourself from your skin?

On our friends' birthdays we meet
and sleep in our back gardens, a ten-man
tent for seven eleven-year-old girls.
We rotate, take turns in the dark to stumble
to the centre of an orbit, pull our trousers down
while the torch light hovers on bare bottoms.

We show the secret of self to each other,
a flash of the body we are told to keep
hidden, aliens under observation,
searching for ourselves outside,
we play hide-and-seek in the black holes
of all those unseen.

We are an afterglow of nebular children.
The moon, just as young, blushes
all the colours she is usually fist-
fighting autumn for. After all, it's hard to find
ourselves whole when always looking
for more than what we have become.

Search parties out. Beams shine, stadiums flood,
the rotate of a disco ball, light
filtering through the transparency
of tracing paper. I see those girls in the mirror
of my changing reflection like the mood-rings
we wear middle-finger proud.

Those 'I love you's saved for
someone special, as if

conversing in birthday song,
we started swapping in conversation
that night. The absolute brightness of light
brave enough to charge us all.

Until we stopped searching
for someone to speak of that
acceptance, louder than the sound
of ourselves singing,
every candle blowing oration
around the sun.

IN THE CINEMA WITH MY UNCLE

We watch as a tiny girl in a tutu
spins around her home,

bashing ornaments off tables
into bits. My uncle whispers,

'She's like you were as a child,'

and I smile remembering the flight
of hummingbird wings

and explosions of myself, limbs
lifted cloud-bound, until he adds,

'A chubby thing trying to be a ballerina.'

The cinema collapses in
until it is just me

and my skeleton, counting bones.

MY AUNT MARIA

In a uniform of dirt, plaits
threaded to her scalp and socks
rolled to the knees, she runs

to school as if betterment
were chasing her – my Aunt Maria.
She once skipped but has started

to drag her father's name behind,
until she keeps tripping over
her own past. Fast behind,

the other children wring
out the words 'jailbird's daughter'
like a wet towel.

He was locked away
when Aunt Maria was a half-moon,
buffing and fusing in the vastness

of her mother's stomach.
Some days he shoots
words up to the sky, a wish

that she will forgive him.
When his sentence ends
Aunt Maria is eight.

She goes to Dartmoor
to see her father for the first time.
She thinks about running into his

silence, the weight of that cord a tug
of return, yet it strangles like a noose
and she stays still, blinking out day

from behind the break of her mother's heart.
When he's close and she catches his face
in the opposite of hers, crying hardship,

bravely breaching the world like she once had,
Aunt Maria cuts the invisible
cord, leaves it on the ground raw

and bloody for the next inmate to collect,
and takes the hand of her father home,
swollen with all the words never sent.

ACHOO

_____

When I sneeze I hear my father's sneeze.
Strange how we carry another life in the hospital
of our bodies. Like my father had his mother's

laugh, spontaneous as a cough, and his father's
unspoken guilt, until there was nothing but a backlog
of apologies caught in our family's mouths.

WRECKAGE

I have a memory.

Age six I came home
to find the cracked ceiling
of our kitchen open,
the floorboards flooded,
bath collapsed through,
the bathroom a tsunami
at our feet.

My father sat
in the aftermath of
plaster and puddles,
doubled over, head held
in his palms.

It was the first time
I had ever seen
his face contort.
I thought it was the wreck
of our kitchen
until I climbed aboard his lap
and he mouthed,
'On top of everything else,
this morning your grandfather died.'

My father has a memory.

Swimming in the ocean,
floating on his dad's
stomach, the milky sky
a storybook above them both.
'I have to go the
pub now,' his father spoke,
and left his son treading
the surface, keeping his head
above all that water, trying
desperately not to drown.

THE EMPEROR SHADOW-BOXES
AS THE BONES OF OUR WOMEN
GROW STRONGER

My grandfather died when I was six years old and the last thing I remember about him was his penis. It dangled like a heavy sigh, this alien part of my grandfather's body, shrivelled and helpless. He'd just had a heart attack and begun taking the tubes out, tugging at thick rubber stoppers from his arms so he could stand up and walk around that old Victorian hospital naked. We tried to stop him, pulled blankets around his shoulders and shouted for help, but there is only so much you can do to stop a dying man from living the way he wants to.

Tommy Tantony was his name. He owned bars and boxing rings. A villain, violent and powerful. 'I give young men a purpose,' he would say, not like in his time – a youth spent lost and wandering with nothing to fight for. Yet he cast a dark shadow in our family, as if he were an opaque object blocking out any chance of light. Through the years that flooded from underneath him, he carried the heavy weight of that darkness, and stumbled through life blind to the gentleness of what each moment might bring. I remember looking over towards my father during that day of nakedness and dying, wondering how it must have been to see the Godfather to all who stepped into the ring wear a face so familiar, yet carry the heart of a stranger.

In his last weeks and months, my grandfather asked to go on picnics with us all. He laughed more and stopped smoking. I wonder if he wanted to taste cleaner air then. He had never been so soft towards us until those moments where he knew he was leaving it all behind, when he was no longer having to make his mark on the world. It was like he closed his eyes in order to see, like he became transparent as the light passed straight through all that dark.

THE OCEAN

One hundred and ninety-three people drowned when the *Herald of Free Enterprise* sank in 1987. The passenger ferry departed the Belgian port of Zeebrugge only to capsize twenty-three minutes later; the bow doors had been left open and water filled the ship. It sank, a whisper of cargo on the bed of the ocean. At the lip of the surface drowned bodies emerged, pulled back to shore by the magnet of land. My father was working on that ship, had left it just that morning and was at home that night when the news came into our house like a tidal wave, when his close friends were named amongst the dead, when the many pathways of chance and possibility crashed together and said, 'You have done it again, you blagger, escaped the pain that is so rightfully yours.'

I had just turned two, he was thirty and he held me close to his chest like another heart.

Aged eight, Pegwell Bay, we were swimming together, Thomas, Dad and I. The horizon was to be conquered and my body thought itself capable of anything somehow. I had gone under before, saved by two strangers and returned to my sobbing mother. This time I was even more determined to keep going. I kicked through the water, my limbs working furiously, taking me further and further out. My father was trying to keep Thomas afloat, hands grasping both sides of my brother's body. My father couldn't carry on holding me back. Perhaps he didn't want to; perhaps even then he knew I would heed the call of the old siren song over any other.

A wave swept over me and I was under. I scrambled for the surface only to be borne back by the current. My mouth opened and shut, the salty water flooded my inside. I was dangling in the sea, my body heavy, that world of air and land suddenly so distant I became convinced it was no longer worth trying to reach it. When my next out-breath came it was calmer. The weight lifted from my head as a darkness descended and in that moment, aged eight, I knew death was inevitable and that there was something to be found in accepting that.

Then my father's hands plunged through the dark mass of water above, pulled me into the air, spluttering and gasping. With two children stapled to his body like armbands, he swam back to the shore and we collapsed onto the mottled stones. He didn't shout at me this time.

My father's best friend was killed when the *Herald* sank. I ask him how he handled it.

'I was the lucky one,' he says, 'the one that got away. Think of the family of the dead. Or the ones who survived the accident but were left with the misery of experiencing so much trauma.'

'Did you transfer to another ship afterwards?'

'Yeah. It was never the same, though. This darkness stayed with us all. We didn't laugh any more. I think my depression started around that time.'

I sit in silence, the phone wedged against the sharp bone of my shoulder. For a while, I listen to his breathing.

'Do you think it could be related?' I ask.

There is a long, held pause before he says, 'I never thought of that,' and goes quiet again.

Seabirds cry. Air casts out forgotten shipwrecks forever held inside the bony skin of seashells; I can taste water swallowed in gallons. I can hear the memory of an upturned past whistling somewhere.

SPILT MILK

Mother's arthritic hands spill
the milk as Fadumo swears
good luck. 'That's what we say
in Somalia, if you knock over
something white all possible
futures come to your rescue.'

There is twenty years' difference
between us. Aged thirty, fifty
and seventy-three, there are wars
that both my mother and Fadumo
have survived, have swapped
for migration and longing.

There are hearts pulled across
countries, friends folded,
the world of blood and bone
to learn from. After the milk
has been spilt, we tell a woman
not to cry for what has been lost –

but she will mourn regardless,
sometimes in secret, sometimes
into the throat of another.
She will unlearn the holding of her
tongue, the softening of those stiff lips,
she will ache.

LAURA NETTLESHIP

He found her in the East End of London, my mother's mother. White as an egg, mouth red as fruit, she was not like him – his liquorice face, those eggplant lips, were such a shock. When he asked to walk her across the street he whispered, 'I won't touch you. I just want to be close.' Laura Nettleship blushed in a way he never could. 'I'm nothing special,' she said, and he laughed at her mistake.

They were married in secret four months later. When they were alone he ran his hands over her body, tracing the shape of Gambia, Senegal, Cape Town from one shoulder blade to the other. Laura Nettleship climbed inside his shadow, followed his body as if it were her own. She noticed duality, the opposition of everything, and she had never seemed so translucent as she did when she was next to him.

From their apartment she watched England move. Hardworking men sold fish, colourful young girls skipped hand-in-hand, the alchemy of a city happened beneath their bedroom window. Inside the four walls, inside their introversion and escape, she cooked joints of lamb, roasted potatoes, washed the glasses he sucked the last dregs of whisky from.

'We've found home,' she'd say, pressing her mouth on his.

They had five children together in four years. Her brother lived just outside the city, in a house built on stilts on top of a river. There they did English things together: ate eggs laid by bulging hens, floated lazily across the river through sunrises and sunsets.

'Tell me about Grandad's land,' Maggie, their eldest, asked as those long hours began to fall away, and he wove together moments: maize fields and diplomacy, snake bites and ocean liners, bleeding suns and bulging black beans.

'Stop talking magic,' Laura Nettleship would say. On those tired, heavy days. Those all-too-familiar days where she slept in until afternoon. Where the curtains were drawn to remove the light. Where his touch would do nothing to wake her.

When he drank too much or talked of Africa like it was the only thing he'd ever learned to love, Laura Nettleship disappeared. It was all the things she never knew, never reached: explosions of fruits never tasted, relentless sun beating the backs of her calves, the bravery and perseverance of a whole continent of people. On the lead-up to their separation she wore gold, neon-coloured dresses, cooked with spices whose names she couldn't pronounce.

When he left, she tried making herself fatter. Africa was big, after all; she was plump and bulging with life. But Laura Nettleship was all bones by then, all sunken eyes and aching.

She started giving away her children. She thought the fewer she had, the easier it would be to provide for them. First Henry went to her mother, Oscar to a great-aunt and then finally, one day, she walked to the local orphanage and just left them there. Leah was five, Maggie was eight and Ruth wasn't even one, yet she stayed quietly in Maggie's arms, all folded up like a map.

SUMMER

When we were younger, during one of those dry-heat summers, Mum put a paddling pool out in the garden. We played in it all day, the sun a blister above us. When it became cooler in the late afternoon, we told my father we were cold, and so he dressed us in jumpers and trousers and placed us back in the paddling pool.

I was always so grateful that the fun never ended when he was around, but I rarely understood his choices. Two children tugging at the attention of our overworked parents. Truthfully, I'm not sure if those dance routines were made for anyone but him. The twirling batons and backflips. All the high-top ponytails and side-stepping in time to the mess of that broken cassette player. Even the rebellions, the bedroom where I sat by the window sending smoke signals to the sun, the evenings I ran away to philosophers dressed as gang leaders (make-believe warriors on pretend horseback). My clenched teeth and fluttering heart.

There was a time when we didn't speak for years, though those silences always were full of sentences somehow. My father's words would come to me in odd moments, when I was arguing with some boyfriend or other, and I tied those conversations we once shared together and wore them like a rosary in front of my heart.

This morning I call him. He's living in a one-bedroom housing association flat now, ten minutes' walk from the place he had called home for thirty years. Home: old soul records, torn Martin Luther King posters and tins crammed full of broken biscuits. We make a plan to meet; a pilgrimage from my house to his. In the car, we speak in small-talk until he says, 'Sorry your relationship has ended,' and I snap and say something that the seven-year-old girl in my ribcage means, the one who spits: 'But you didn't know how to love me either, did you?' It is not me speaking. Not this thirty-year-old woman who has practised words with kindness and meaning. We drive on in silence, regressing, growing younger. At one point he pulls up to a cashpoint and takes £50 out, walks back to the car, sits down and awkwardly hands me the notes.

'I thought you could buy something. Cheer yourself up.'

I know this is his way of saying: *I do care but the words get lost, and the emotions are strange, and you are something I never learned to understand. Here, this is a thing that is tangible.*

We stay still. I tell him the stories I remember from childhood, exams and alleyways scrawled with the ink of our surnames. I tell him about the books I'm reading now, Ram Dass quotes and journeys back home. He speaks of old cities burned to the ground, a metaphor, he says, for starting over again.

As we sit I notice all the small things around me. The newsagent's where he buys his paper. The bench I used to eat chips on. The way the sun smacks the glass. It seems easy once more. Like there was never anything here or there, lost or found, between us now.

CHANGE

My mother left my father when she was seventy and over the year that followed we walked more together, she and I.

We watch the months turn into their fullness, the colours infiltrate the trees, the landscape bloom or decay. Those cyclical patterns of beginning and end.

'Do you remember when we all went on holiday to Crantock, stayed in that bungalow?' she says. 'Your father loved the sea. Before you were born we went to a Stevie Wonder concert in Brighton and missed the last bus back, so we slept on the beach. Sometimes I think, why didn't we just stay in a hotel? But it was exciting, bundled up together like a pile.'

Now the golden months of autumn envelop us. The leaves are browning or fading, skeletons of veins bulging through their transparency, the half-kept wishes of decomposing dandelions at our feet.

'We would have some great dinner parties,' she says, her face seeming to soften. 'I remember once I cooked Italian cod and mini-lasagnes for a starter and we drank and danced while you two were sleeping upstairs. I didn't have a dishwasher then and it took us two hours to wash up together. But that was the best part of the evening somehow. I made him a bread pudding for his birthday last week. I almost wanted to say, "Shall we wash up the dish at my house, for old times' sake?"'

The tangles of blackberries at the side of the road have begun to bruise. I don't ever remember my parents arguing. Over time I just watched them change.

'I didn't, though. I just took the dish back and washed it myself. There were so many phone calls offering condolences for my failed marriage. Two children created, houses moved in and out of. Thirty years of marriage, working out who you are in unison with another. Holidays. Tragedies. Triumphs. Now, I don't see how any of that can be seen as failure.'

Occasionally, a gold light smashes through the grey sky and soaks us with warmth. I hold her hand and it shakes silently in mine as we walk across the fields, a stone's throw from where home keeps promising to be.

HERE

_____

I search for home in another. I move a bed onto his tongue, a curtain rail along his spine, at his feet I lay a rug. It is never for long. Before the price of rent becomes unbearable, I am searching again for the next reason to leave.

FORMLESS

We were in a room that hadn't been cleaned
properly in years, cellophane windows
and tired smells, slept in a single bed,
multiplied ourselves in Petri dishes,
clever enough to keep the outside at bay.

We made love again, as if our bodies depended
on all that feeling, pressed together like dead
daffodils in books, full up, and golden
on one another's skin.

Unknowingly we broke condoms,
muttered prayers,
kept goodbyes for the morning and
knew that night was meant
to be swallowed into the pit of us.

You were made formless,
us frightened by the thought of you
growing inside me like an ache,
a question mark, shaped like a secret.

I discovered you in a Wetherspoon's toilet,
pissed on a static test and received
positive feedback, two months already of
heaving the weight of you around.

And the reason I had to get you out early
wasn't because I couldn't wait any longer.
I just didn't know how to make
all of you into something
lasting.

I care for you more now than I ever
could have then. I watch you
through the kaleidoscope
of my friends' growing offspring,
the memory banks of my teenage years,
and somewhere between cloud
and clock hands, if only for an instant.
I understand what it is to love
something to death.

THE BALLOON

He is pulled towards her like a child at a fairground. Something about all that lust she has for living, those weak handshakes tucked away in her pockets, that heart that keeps spontaneously combusting. He says, 'You are so full of life, you're like a balloon. I have never seen the world so vibrant, so alive, as I do with you.' For a while he forgets himself, but she never wanted that. Never wanted a ghost of what he had been before, yet he seems to float so transparent in her world, until suddenly he has disappeared completely. She doesn't notice at first. So used to his body breathing in bed next to her own. But he has gone, the relationship so vast he became lost in their love. Or perhaps in holding on so tight to the balloon of her he floated away. She tries to find him again. Is he hiding under the bed? Has he camped out behind her earlobe, is that his voice whispering? She blames herself. Of course she does; no one wants a woman who will turn her lover into air. Yet she only wanted his eyes, his nose, the fleshy body to hold – thick and full – his mouth crammed with ideas. She only ever wanted all of him. To learn how weightless they could be together.

I'VE MOVED MY BED

in between the bookcase
and window,
inches from where
the earth of us began.

In between the prayers before sleep
muttering you back,
I spat and shook your name
from my heart.

In between words, you still get caught
in my conversations; in between now
and eight months before,
I still wear this ache.

In between the turn
of day's light into the husk
of this evening,
I see you hide sometimes –

in the back of
wrecked nightclubs,
on the smiles of other men,
while in between time – I still carry

the haunt of our bodies together.

A LATE NIGHT EXPERIMENT

Sun's sunk, the earth's tilting turning on the
arc of itself; outside the moon is weary,
heavy it sits in all that light. Yet here in
this room, we sleep awake. You inside me,
me inside you, like a never-ending
mirror hall. While our bodies tangle together,
electrons separate in all directions,
I exist somewhere else, still dreaming his skin.
'Will you write about this?' you whisper,
while I try to observe you, try to gather
the sky, wishing on stars so far away
they are long dead. To shoot him back to me,
like I've read those particle guns keep on
shooting all hope into infinity.

FORGET THE BREAK OF OUR HEARTS

*Henry Molaison, known by thousands of psychology students as
'HM', had his memory removed on an operating table in a
hospital in Hartford, 1953. He was twenty-seven years old.*

At twenty-seven years old I tell my friends
that I want to withdraw him from memory
as if some moment best forgotten.
They say, 'Remember the good,'

but the good has been gagged and bound,
weighted with stones and rolled from the banks.
I try to paddle out but I'm stuck in
the same moment of regret,

resurrecting memories of him as if shipwrecks
dragged to the surface. I need to sink the future
but I don't know how to forget
all that doesn't drown.

Don't know how to remove the tender times
that bob and float from the outside in.
Don't know how to forget that love still sits
marooned in the depths of me.

*

On the edge of the cerebral cortex they cut
the seahorse-shaped hippocampus inside
Henry's skull. In the cup of his hands he holds
every possible past. Rips away the afternoons

spent curled inside the question mark of his lover's
body, the evenings drunk and firing arguments
like darts under the swell of the moon. Pulls at whole
months screaming goodbyes at one another, his hands buried

in the tangle of her hair. On waking he tries to configure
her face out of dreams, but her lips fade,
teeth disintegrate, tongue evaporates into air –
her features fall from mind like rain.

Now, when asked what he remembers he says,
'Nothing,' and when asked, 'Well, what
is the point in living?' he replies, 'To be of service
to those around me. To love without condition.'

NOW

The property of a past, look ahead, there are infinite reasons to stay. Pull the blinds up, let the light flood in. Your hands spread all the summer out of me; this winter will be short.

THE SHIP

That night we had been drinking. Stuffing jerk chicken into our stomachs, cajun pepper stuck under the half-moons of our fingernails. Swinging like a needle around the compass of the city – Bristol at night – tangled up in the pulse of that place like strands of seaweed entwined around itself. We walked for hours, navigating through the streets, finding naughty in everything. He picked up traffic cones and placed them in a circle around me whilst I sang a Smashing Pumpkins song into a makeshift microphone. I photographed him in the half-light of shopfronts as he stared blankly at lace-up boots and mannequins. We found adventure, floating between the ordinary of a place so known and the unfamiliarity of exploring it together.

We walked to the top of the Christmas steps and he clambered onto a skip.

'Come aboard,' he shouted down as if it were a ship.

Stepping over the mountain of unwanted, I pulled myself up and over, scratching elbows on unseen things, disused and void. Smelt the putrid rawness of our new voyage and found his hand somewhere amongst the rubble. We collapsed starboard, tongues urgent and hands awake. I remember how gently my fingers ran over his skin, slippery with the residue of chicken. He unzipped my dress, my backbone laid out like holiday plans, his fingers clever. The moon was a camera above us and my skirt was caught between his fingers. I remember how our fucking felt like the christening of something. Champagne bottles smashed against the side of a bow, ready to set sail.

MOTHER TONGUE

———————

Just before you part me in the middle like a hairline,
before you lay your heart to the chest of my mattress,

you kneel in between my legs and clasp your hands
together in prayer. Your eyes flutter open and shut,

shut and open, rolling Spanish r's on repeat, you begin
to press a secret into me. An hour passes through us,

winding me up like a clock face. I backfire and snap
back, your mouth fills me with promises.

Spit and saliva converse, translate the unknown
of one another's skin into something speakable.

An intercourse of language can be heard in here,
that only our flesh understands.

THE THREE FACES OF WOMANHOOD

Are you satisfied with my body?
With this butcher's-table rib-rack chest,
the hunger of these bovine
stomachs, my inferno heart?

Do the streaks along my hips
please you? Cracks on leather
hide, the torn tendons of life
stretching for more.

Are you satisfied with my body?
The way my freckles barbecue
when sun-bruised, milk parlour
breasts crying spilt, the changing

minutes in which I wear myself older.
This body was once tiny teeth
and the first small hold of acne
gathered in flocks on my cheeks.

This body became an abattoir
of growing pains, cyclical months
that never came round easy; this body
compared itself to sucked-in bone-

sad-men's-mag front-page spread.
This body didn't always know how to fit.
There is a child still inside of me, a teenager
milking the distance of my spine,

an elder waiting patiently to bloom.
This body's started collecting lines
to wear trophy-proud, silver and grey
will emerge one day, the alchemy of flesh evolves.

For now this body is a woman
trying to dress as if finished
while those three females decay
and dream inside my skin.

THE POET AND THE CHEF

You bring me paella in Tupperware
and wine from Catalan. Ten hours
later we are scrambling eggs
in my kitchen, brewing coffee

while our fairy-cake eyes flutter
between one another's mouths.
We should do this until the end, I say,
swallowing six years of friendship.

Yes, you laugh, the poet and the chef;
we both know the way to the heart after all.
First course you began to knead
the folds of my flesh, tasted me

across the ridges of your tongue.
Second course, I whispered all the
ways in which dessert could be served.
It's poetry, I said, but you just laughed,

pulled me further into the recipe of us.
Third course we boiled, baked,
tasted, licked. Slapped, steamed,
roasted, fried, wrote out the menu

of our artichoke hearts, while I
wanted to throw up and digest you.
There is everything left to say when
both full and empty at once.

THE BIG–SMALL CITY

Every time I think of loving
someone again, I build a city
in my heart.

I fill the city with noise and bustle.
Men old enough to know better
drink pints, women exchange words
as children play, dogs bark,
you can't hear yourself think in there.

When ready, I open this city out and say,
'This place is busy,
there are skyscrapers and banks.
There's hopscotch roads
stuffed with traffic,
delicatessens with fancy cheese,
and cafés with beautiful twenty-somethings
shooting espressos.

In this city there's a second-floor
apartment with fading walls,
cigarette ends and a double bed.
Sprawled on the sheets, I'm there,
waiting for someone to come home.'

FADO

In a room pumped with people
we listen to the heart sing
in a tongue strange to our ears.
Longing to survive, it thuds with ache,

and I miss you even though you sit
by my side, tracing futures on my skin.
Imagine: a teenage girl cutting
her heart into pieces, us swallowing

endocardium, her body, her song;
giving us the kiss of life, mouth-to-mouth,
she presses lips to our chests until
our ribcages rattle and her voice packs

this room with promise. The music fills us
with a giddy torture. You and I hold
on to one another, knowing that this
is the last night for a while that our

fingers will bolt, our limbs amalgamate,
and when you cry, unashamedly,
hearing the song of the Portuguese people,
I trip and fall in love over and over again.

EXECUTION

A man on death row chooses
one last meal, pleads for a knife,
fork, plate, a single black
olive and nothing more.

His favourite food, perhaps?
Or a prayer. Stout knowledge
that it only takes a pip, a seed,
a stone, to grow new life again.

I am at the end of one relationship
and start of another. My heart,
locked in the grove of my body,
travels whole countries to meet

your mouth. In Portugal, we sit
next to an olive tree and I
consider the penalty of love.
At times, I have done wrong.

I pull a branch; forgiveness is a past
left buried in the prison of time. So,
let us feed, pick hope with fingers
and dine on our future.

LOST

How do you break the silence and begin the first moment of introduction to those different from you? The voice, the voice is the instrument.

THE VOICE, THE SOUND, THE SONG

*England's education secretary Nicky Morgan has rejected MPs'
calls to make sex-and-relationship education compulsory in all
schools.*

BBC News, 11th February 2016

1

A congregation of girls rattling
like tambourines were once played
in the back of cars. Detached
dance-hall tracks and the reek
of aftershave choked. While the boys
sweated some kind of love-language
hard to swallow, those girls kept cotton wool
in their mouths, stuffed ears with fingers,
thought of themselves erupting into song
but remained silent –
convinced they needed someone
else's tongue to make them sing.

*

Where did he learn to roll over
and welcome the moon in so quickly?
While she's still wide-eyed
and waiting for a crescendo
to rush her skin, an orchestra
of high and low notes to lift
her skywards like a hymn.

Where did she learn that sex
was nothing but the tune
of repentance? The waltz
of his hands so quick to start
and stop. When did the break
of her heart turn into a love
song writing its own end?

A congregation of boys blowing
like trumpets were once played
in the back of cars. Detached
dance-hall tracks and the reek
of perfume choked. While the girls
sweated some kind of love-language
hard to swallow, those boys bit
their lips broken, kept their eyes glazed,
thought of themselves erupting into song
but remained silent –
convinced they needed someone
else's tongue to make them sing.

*

Where did she learn to roll over
and shut out the sun, while he practised
a duet solo? A role created
from online videos.
Where did he learn that a maestro
plays a lonely longing
on the backbone of him?

Voice breaks with age
from countertenor to bass,
yet he still stays misunderstood.
Why did he think that sex
was nothing but the slow dance
of her leaving?

*

Never taught the whole note
of skin, never taught the fine tuning
of fingers across flesh, the treble of pleasure,
the rhythm of two equal humans
moving through the scales of each
other's voices.

BAPTISM

She's on her knees at the altar.
It has been a long time coming,
the naming of herself as His child.
Told that all the good
girls go to heaven, before

plunging, before dipped under,
breath forgotten,
she prays that someone
will be there
to save her from drowning.

She's been told God resides within.
She wants Him to appear
as a woman, to emerge
as urgent as the water
that drenches, rusts

and alchemises fluids. But all
she can feel is the presence of a man
she doesn't know.
Looking up to Our Father,
who art distant,

who art a grafter, who art so high above
bruising the sky clear.
Pulled back to the surface
she feels the run
of the priest's fingers as they pass over.

As he pulls her into his chest
like another heart,
she whispers between floating
and sinking,
ashamed of her own lips,

and while the water dries,
she turns her eyes to the ground,
understanding now.
God will always be a single
mother, undressing

for a man's world,
trying to wash herself clean.

THE BROTHEL

Those dogs danced in packs,
barked in a chorus of ugly noise,
yet their puppy eyes made the most
wicked of those men good.

Their job was to stay loyal when
those men exploded, when they kicked
their ribs broken, when they whistled
'Bitch' down from their windows.

After, those men would reach out,
run their fingers through their hair,
wonder if they'd realise
it was their need of them
that frightened the most.

They tried to keep them close.
Had them on leads,
choked their whines into silence,
but there was too much
wandering in those beasts,
too much wild
for those men to tame.

He was a hungry man with twenty
dirty mouths to feed: chained-
up queens howling blue murder,
their need for escape
an alarm bell ringing.

So he let them go.
He thought they would return,
come back whimpering,
eyes lowered, whining for food,
begging for touch.
But they just kept running.

WHERE THE SKIN FITS

———————

I squeezed myself into the body of a woman this morning.
Zipped up my spine like a sin, hoping this skin wouldn't appear
in need of cleaning. I jump-started my heart from the bonnet
of my neighbour's car. These eyes saw similes in everything.
Compare them to a boxing ring; my pupils played out loss on repeat.
Laugh with me, I cried. I promise not to take it so seriously.
Promise to shrug off the catcalls and wolf-whistles like an animal
sheds when it no longer needs to carry the burden of self.
Promise to bend at the knees, fall short of my dreams; forever
pray to matter and bone, youth and time.

IT'S A DOG'S LIFE

The suicide rate for men is now three and a half times that
of women.

The Guardian, 20th February 2014

Go on boy, fetch a stick, break
a bone, names hurt.
The woodland drizzled wet that day,
bone-bag hanging heavy.
Did those branches snap
your neck, a broken song?
Swing-dancing the space
between sky and earth like that.

When the walker found you,
did he let go of his dog's lead
or retract dear life into a fist?
Did he loosen the collar, in his own
high-pitched scream say,
'Go on, run,' or did he tug and tug
until the thing could barely breathe?

Did he gather the dog
into his chest, synchronised
hearts singing a whistle?
Or did the dog roll over,
play dead, as the walker swallowed
a call, stared up at you
tick-tocking the air,
that strange thing around your throat?

Did the dog snarl,
froth mad, did the walker
smooth its insides gentle
again, say, 'Curl onto the end
of my bed and dream'?

Or did they both howl despair,
this desolate ache
from the furthest point of themselves?
'Sit, lie down, fetch, stop whining.'
Until choice became a sky-walk
under the weight of that tree.

SKELETON

It was late when my friend died
and I remember thinking that even
the night sky had turned violent.
Punch-up stars and a round
bruised moon staring down.

I remember the blackberries
in the shock of streetlights,
the day-old daddy longlegs
stumbling like drunks at our feet,
knowing that soon the sun would follow
and their quick lives would be over.

We walked the skeleton of
streets together that night, after
the trapped air, a phone call
swallowing our mouths,
when we were told his heart
had folded in on itself
like an origami epitaph.

WINTER

Freedom has become a forbidden word in Syria. All around buildings are disintegrating into matter, people are dying – not in that soft passing-into-sleep way, but through the projections of nightmares. Bashar's name chimes around the city of Tartous like an alarm ringing a wake-up call.

She met her husband on a demonstration against the president's regime. He was a Palestinian man with the same understanding of peace as she had: equality and freedom in everyday life. Their relationship was a unity, he saw unknown walkways in her skin, a soundscape of a country being pulled apart by other people's cruelty – it was much like his own country. Their sameness and difference merged them together.

Rima became the poster girl of the Syrian people, bold and willing to say what everyone else needed to hear. Her words were spoken without restraint; she wouldn't settle for destruction. When she was thrown in prison for disagreeing with the president, her husband looked after their two children. Each day he counted the seconds since she had been taken. He found himself walking through a dark silence, not knowing if she would emerge alive. Sometimes she would phone, and they all crammed around his mobile shouting 'I love you's like rapid gunfire.

Their two boys looked for her in everything. 'She is a strong woman,' he told them, 'stronger than me.'

One day, perhaps five weeks after she first disappeared, there was a bang on the door and he swung it open to find her stood there, thinner than before. They collapsed into one another. The children screamed and climbed over their bodies as if they were mountains. For a week they drank glasses of maroon-coloured wine, chain-smoked cigarettes and cradled each other like teenagers do: her hands on his cheek, his arms wrapped around her back, keeping her firmly in place.

They had to flee Syria; it was too dangerous to stay. So they passed through Beirut, Amman to reach Paris, where they stayed.

At night they listened to Arabic music and dreamed of home. 'I miss our lemon tree,' their children said. Yet the further away from the struggle Rima was, the more she suffered. The motion sickness caused by moving had shaken her into a stranger. The echo inside herself held an unknown woman, a partner, a mother, unsure of what she was fighting for. They began to argue, tiny conflicts at first which escalated into explosions. Their four walls in Paris became a new prison and anxiety attacked late at night as they lay back-to-back in bed. Their own battle was in silence. It was in the raised eyebrows and awkwardbody language, arms folded over stomachs. They gazed out of windows instead of staring into the honesty of each other's faces. Two thousand and seven hundred miles from the destruction of Syria they searched for home in those long, disappointing days. Spat lemon pips into space and wondered if anything might grow.

THE INEVITABLE FALL

into a strange new place means landing
heart-side-up. Means a stomach sick
with someone else's past, speaking in
a language heavy with hate.

It's once belonging to your body,
now too ashamed to keep walking it
proud through the city we felt
held us all. It's a referendum

in favour of difference, the crack and pull
apart of yolk and egg-white. It's a home
built from the calculus of division
– shutting them out, shutting us in.

SONNET FOR A LONELY PLANET

how do you speak for a world whose tongue
is dust-dry whose lungs have turned
into the cremation of cities whose face
is the exploding landscape of Lebanon
revealing jaw dislocated whose bones
are Syria's skeleton deformed
I do not know what ears the bombs in Palestine
need to be heard by or how to stop Nigeria's eyelids
from shutting out all chance of light
why does Earth's skin need only stretch
over the bones of those humans
protecting the tiny heart that breaks
with every blow to the body
that our huge world keeps suffering

COMMANDMENTS

Forget the boats that bowed and sagged
under the weight of us migrating from war.
Keep the faces of our poorest people distant.
Don't recall the colonising of someone
else's home or the ossein of slaves
our cities were built upon.

Remember the language forced down
the throats of those who spoke in other.
Remember the good old days,
pubs clear of black skin and Irish chatter,
our mouths loaded with shame.
Forget all the fucking that made us,

the dirt of Scilly and filth of Cape Town,
the Romani gypsy that travels the architecture
of our nervous system, the land our great
grandparents loved before they ran,
faces downcast from the sun's warning.
And when forgotten, start to make new again –

build a country from words so weak
they break with utterance, a people
afraid of how a stranger mimics
their dreams. Finally, form a future
from the white noise of a history
best kept forgotten.

EXCHANGE

———————

Of this: money kept me quiet, my head crammed
with holidays I could never quite afford to take.

Money turned the upright of my back into a collapsed empire,
loaded my politicians with substance – fat and full with more.

Money spun the yarn over my eyes, didn't know how to keep
its lips pursed, money was always shouting its worth through

fancy foods. We fought like cats and dogs, snarled at one another
from the white cliffs of our teeth, spitting pennies out for miles.

I tried to live without money, but money kept saving my life;
kept pumping my stomach, quenching my thirst. I hated money.

I hated it like a working-class girl, cardiac sick with worry
that she might not make the rent this month. I love money.

I love it like the emergence of a middle-class woman, wearing a dress
bought to dance with abundance, under the rich, golden sky.

FAR

I've tried swallowing the entire world before, digested every country I have entered, my mouth filled with Venice, Split, Fez, Berlin. I have learnt to say goodbye in seven different languages. Au revoir, adiós, ciao, adjö, hamba kahle, عادو, tchau.

THE CALL TO PRAYER

Mogadishu was the first place
I heard the Call to Prayer; my friend
named it the Allah song as goosebumps
bombed my skin. That night,
in her apartment we cooked spiced

paprika from the market,
curls of chorizo from Madrid,
okra from Sudan – the pans were filled
with flavours, then fried until
the sizzle stuffed our ears.

She turned on the radio, a thump of sound.
We began to dance ourselves
giddy to the pop songs from home.
When the Call to Prayer spilt
in from the city outside, sprinkled our music

with undertones of the ancients,
ritual became us revolving around that
kitchen in unison. We prepared
an ecstatic offering and hungrily prayed
with the soles of our feet.

WHAT DID I FIND IN ALL THOSE PLACES?

Two prayer beads, a blessing from a Sufi master,
three holiday romances, six bad tummies,
nine hundred bottles of water, twenty unforgettable
train journeys, a dead baby floating
in the Ganges, two dodgy eggs in Delhi,
one argument on a Mexican beach,
one breakup on a South Indian beach,
an orgasm in the stomach of the Grand
Canyon, sixty-two postcards from anywhere
but here, all the journeys I never took, one
knife-fight in a San Franciscan subway,
a leaf from the tree Buddha found
enlightenment under, total clarity
in a service station outside of Hull.

THE GAY PRIDE RALLY OF ISTANBUL

It was the summer my heart was an explosion.
The summer that tear gas leaked like a secret.
He showed me the tattoo of Jesus on his arm
and I realised we were both willing to do anything
to make God a part of us.

I'd just watched the Whirling Dervishes spin dizzy,
stumbled into the gay pride rally of Istanbul
and found ecstasy
in everything, found heaven
in the soundtrack of disco
and holy rage in technicolour flags.

Found him, ripping a kebab into confetti
as conversation rolled out from our tongues,
like a prayer mat uncurled.

He told me his wife and child
were still behind trying to live
in the remains of Damascus, while he
searched for a home somewhere safer,
counting the countries he had passed
through on one wish.

A Muslim man,
trying to enter the Orthodoxy of Greece,
keeping courage close,
he pointed to his tattoo and said,
'On crossing through the border
your god saved my skin.'

The soundtrack of freedom got stuck
when the police used rubber bullets on us,
their shields as battering rams.
It was then we realised
we needed to stop looking
to the sky to save us.

BAKED APRICOTS

I found Allah once.
It was Morocco seven years ago,
my knees collapsed on a prayer mat,
arms flat-packed behind my back,
heart beating like that of a racehorse.
It was thirty-four degrees of hot sun.
Baked apricots, speakers spitting prayers.
Me looking everywhere for God.
Awkward and still, waiting for
the return of my breath.
When suddenly I saw him.
Old now, ninety or so,
bending down and picking up fag butts
and somehow I then knew
he too was trying to bring back
that which you just need to give up.

I found the Guru once.
Outside a gurdwara in Bristol.
She was a woman waiting
in a short skirt and high heels,
four children pulling on every limb,
her still smiling somehow.
It was a dry day
and she spoke to them all
as if she were speaking in scriptures,
promised pack lunches and trips to the parks.
Kindness revealing itself as miracles –
tapping Morse codes across her children's skin,
saying, 'Let me in through every single pore of you.'

I found God once.
Aged nine, St Francis Church, sat between
Emilie Slade and Kimberly Chapman.
It was the assembly first thing; all clapping hands,
we sang old forgotten hymns of birth and stars.
Instead, I looked out the window,
watched wind pass through tree leaves.
Watched the sun spread the sky red,
an ink blot on tracing paper.
Watched nature move together perfectly.

*

Don't just find me on Sundays,
somewhere pious, somewhere forgotten,
quietly timetabling God's entrance.
Turn me into a hymn,
for I will never know silence like I do now.
Playing songs across your gravestone, God,
trying to wake the life out of your peace,
I spent too much time editing
your face out of the black days,
scratching the surface of my heart.

I always thought you were a fairy tale,
a man-made cut-out, a ridiculous promise
that never came true.
But I've seen through you now;
you're standing in the newsagent's,
in the shopkeepers and customers.
In the bus drivers and check-out girls.
In the debt collectors, babysitters
and dinner ladies. You're in the waitress
and the bartender, in my mother's
phone calls. I'm sure you were there too, God,
when I never called my father back.
When I thought the plane would crash.
When I swam out of my depth
and nearly drowned.

I'm sorry I didn't find you before.
I found my expectancy.
I'll rest next to you now, fall asleep and dream
of electricity bringing us back together.
I'll dream of discovering you
in my own tangible way,
amongst my own tangible people.

I'll dream of looking for the sacred
and finding holy in everyone.

GO AWAY CLOSER

I told her I was trying to find myself.
Leaving Bristol in search of answers somewhere
more exotic than this place. I ask for advice.
Try to pull wisdom out of her mouth like teeth.

We scatter ourselves over Easton,
speak of Thailand, India, Nepal, Bhutan. Out there
in those countries where we learn ourselves lost
in another culture. I ache to forget.

The sun blurs all the avenues out of here
before disappearing. I say how boring this place
has become. How strange it will be to return one day,
knowing how it feels to have finally found home.

*

That same evening I go to a photography
exhibition alone. Stare at images of children
in refugee camps, their heads on makeshift pillows,
afraid to sleep because their dreams are stuffed

with wandering. I wonder how tropical the dust
of this earth feels to them. How many postcards
from far away are left unsent. Spirits poured
in shots. How much sex on the beach

has been downed on Greek islands, wine
necked in Calais. Mediterranean cruises ended
overboard. I wonder how long their skin
has carried sun, their backpacks crammed with ghosts.

NEAR

And I needed a new route, a way out of those high-rise afternoons stumbling through the choke of this city. No one was hiding my heart here. Move, walk, shout, face it all together. We divide ourselves up into fractions, until what remains is an infinite number of us lonely and separate.

THE DEATH DANCE IS SILENT

For Lydia

Stuffed into her single North London bed
we talk about fading. Talk about the children
we were meant to make by now.

Stretch our bodies towards the future.
Yawn and let it ring like the eternal note
of a Nina Simone song.

We get up. Eat smashed avocados in a café full
of beards. I buy a pot plant, cup it in my hands while
the sunlight draws it older.

We decide to walk silence into Highgate Cemetery,
swallow our tongues, capsize our boat-eyes
down under. The moss grows in clumps,

the trees spasm and cover the faces
of gravestones. The sky is milk-white, laid out above
all these people that matter:

Saad Saadi Ali the Iraqi Communist leader.
The novelist George Eliot. I see the faint and barely
legible name of Jeremy Beadle,

we walk past Karl Marx and my friend says,
'Bet he would have been angry
that we had to pay four quid to get in here.'

And I ask, who will celebrate us? Who will tattoo
our names across slate as we dissolve into this hectic city,
this loud and busy garden of heroes?

THE CITY MOVES

She's a wreck, the crumble of an empire, the decay of history in her hands.
Her stomach's heavy with chicken wings, with empty vodka bottles and the
remains of last night's reckless. Her arms

stretch towards the edges of out, yet she can never quite reach home. In the
elbows of her there are houses painted in a shock of colours. In her palms
primary-school children plant exotic

fruits, watch as chocolate lilies open and close from fist to prayer.
The tongue of her speaks Hindi, speaks Spanish, Patois, French.
Speaks Urdu, Punjabi, Arabic, Somali. The city, she sits

in cafés, swaps stories of fried okra and kalam polow for cheese and ham
sandwiches and builder's tea the colour of bricks. The streets of her carry
shadows as much as this city, she holds a light.

We are invited to dance in her private parts and this city's legs bend,
her chest expands, filled with the weight of us. Here we breathe in unison.
Remembering how bold and scared we always were,

remembering the particles that connect her body to our own, this transplant
of self to other. Her, this city, she is 30% optimistic, 10% equal, 40% unsure,
20% still searching.

She is the whole body of it all. I cross over her spine like I'm walking
barefoot through my own skin and she pulses and moves like blood.
She has broken jaws, hearts, promises, her lashes flutter time.

This city and I, we make a pact. I promise never to leave in such panic again.
She teaches me how to be brave enough to stay. Ready to build and destroy,
build and destroy.

THE BONE-FIELD

In this moment all versions of me exist. Sometimes I try to catch it, but it's always slipping away – everything's so hard to hold close when the future is forever becoming the past.

People said my parents had a child too old and that's why I was an odd little thing. Aged seven I start collecting the bones of animals seen in the woods and fields surrounding our house. Once found, I bring them back, drag a box over to the 'too high' sink and rinse them in tepid water. When asked why I collect them I say, 'I don't really know.' Some days, depending on how interested the person seems or how comfortable I am in their silences, I add, 'I like how smooth they feel' or 'I like the way they seem to change colour in the light.'

Cornel West says, 'You can't really move forward until you look back.'

When we make love in the first instance I forget his name. So used to someone else's body that it completely escapes me who I am with. Luckily the words come out in a heavy breath of syllables so he never hears another man take his place. The French call an orgasm a little death.

'Fancy a drink?' he asks, and I nod. He walks to the bar, opens up his wallet and realises it's empty. He looks back to the table and tries getting my attention. I'm staring out of the window and see him in the glass on top of my own reflection. Sometimes, when with him, I decrease in age; I seem to sulk when I don't get my own way, withdraw into myself until there is nothing left. Other times I feel so learned, so lived in, so used to the euphoric tragedy of life. I promise, I'm not going to fade with time like all the others.

I am an old lady, bent over, almost forgotten by the rest of my body. Back arched like a laden bough, a slow shuffle to my walking as if I were someone on a country lane with all the time in the world to make my journey. Towards me runs a little girl wearing a polka-dot dress and matching headband. She is so urgent in movement that she trips over her own self. As the distance between us shortens, the picture sharpens into something solid. Her tiny hands – fingers spread wide to feel the rush of air; I smile shyly like I'm preparing my mouth for a first kiss. Now, with only a few steps separating us, the little girl makes a last run towards me and just at the moment of collision, the bang of body hitting body, she collapses onto a nearby dustbin, wheezing, hand pulled tight to her chest, and the old lady, me I think, begins to skip away, singing 'Twinkle, Twinkle, Little Star' without a care in the world; heading towards that place where the old dark and new light meet.

I wonder if when we die we just keep returning to the beginning again and again. Like forgetting my keys every time I step out the door and constantly needing to run home. I wonder if we are already dead and born at once, both corpses and tiny babies filing tax returns, hoovering stairs.

When I'm not searching for bones I think about what I might find next. I imagine walking the breadth of the fields, collecting different ones along the way, until I approach a garden. Here I walk through a gate and find myself surrounded by hundreds of bones, thousands of them. No matter how hard I press they never break, never disintegrate, never snap beneath my feet. There are human bones too; those of my grandparents, those of my still-forming brother, school teachers, friends, even my own bones ended up in this garden somehow. Then I imagine lying across them, body spread outwards, eyes closed, while the bones hold up all the weight of me. If anyone were to ask why I collect them, here in this place, I might answer, 'I think it's something about that moment where we are not quite alive but not quite dead either; still existing but ceasing to be what we were before. Remembered only through the marrow of what we leave behind. Something about old and young becoming the same thing, this hard tissue that seems to defy all time.'

FOUND

How courageous would it be to add our journeys together? Collide and create a future worth heading toward. After all, weren't we always only ever 'walking each other back home?'

Rebecca Tantony

Rebecca Tantony has read in numerous venues, including the Royal Albert Hall, the Natural History Museum, the Arnolfini, St George's, The South Bank Centre and Colston Hall, as well as a scattering of house parties and pub toilets. Her commissioned short stories, journalism, and poetry have been published in various anthologies and magazines and her readings have led her to Turkey, India, Sweden and Italy. As well as being writer in residence in a variety of libraries, schools and art institutes in 2016 Rebecca completed an MA in Creative Writing at Bath Spa University. Since 2017 she has been touring an Arts Council Funded immersive spoken word show under the same title as this collection. When not performing she teaches in multiple venues, including the Barbican Theatre and Royal Geographical Society. In San Francisco, she worked for the globally-recognised creative writing centre 826 Valencia. Most importantly, Rebecca has an obsession with dancehall, singing in the car at traffic lights, drinking wine with the people she loves most in the world, meditation, travel and hanging out with her cat Chicken.

She is the author of Talk You Round Till Dusk *(Burning Eye, 2015).*

www.rebecca-tantony.com

The Voice, The Sound, The Song was previously published in 2016 by Ink, Sweat and Tears.

Baptism and *My Aunt Maria* were previously published in 2017 by Bare Fiction.

Cover artwork by Anna Higgie
www.annahiggie.co.uk

Lightning Source UK Ltd.
Milton Keynes UK
UKHW05f1955131018
330456UK00007B/124/P